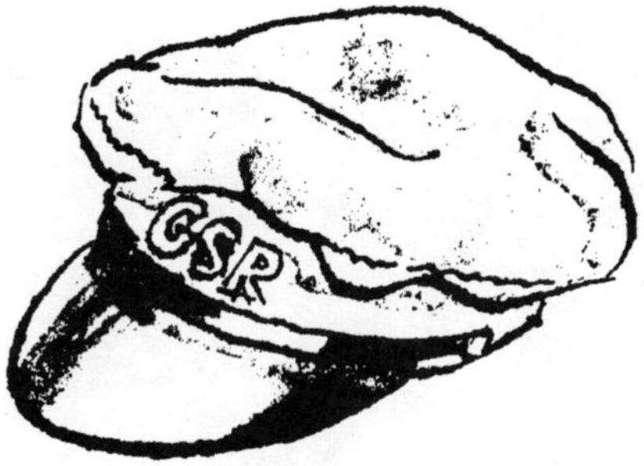
GSR

The Man from the Railway

James P. McNally

A nostalgic and humorous look back
at 50 years in the railway

LOCAL HISTORY COLLECTION
ON STREAM

© James P. McNally

Sketches: Frank Sanquest
Editor: Marie Crowley
Cover photograph: Joe Wilson
Typesetting: Bill Murphy
The Author and On Stream gratefully acknowledge the contribution of photographs from:
Cork Examiner Publications
Mr Walter McGrath
Mr. Joe St. Leger, Irish Railway Records Society
Mr. Joe Wilson, The Wilson Collection
Irish Rail.
Typing for the author: Clare McNally

All rights reserved. No part of this publication may be copied, reproduced or transmitted in any form without the prior permission in writing from the publishers.

Published 1992
by
On Stream Publications.
Cloghroe, Blarney,
Co.Cork. Ireland.
Tel/Fax
353 21 385798

ISBN: 1 897685 99 8

I wish to dedicate this book
to my dear wife Josephine

contents

The job and life in a different era 9

Cobh 23

Youghal 27

The Blarney Tram 31

Donoughmore 32

The Ticket Collector 33

The Crash of '27 36

Looking back at the old stations 38

Joe, Jimmy and Jack 44

The Specials 46

The War Years 53

Engines on the line 55

Characters and anecdotes of the Railway 58

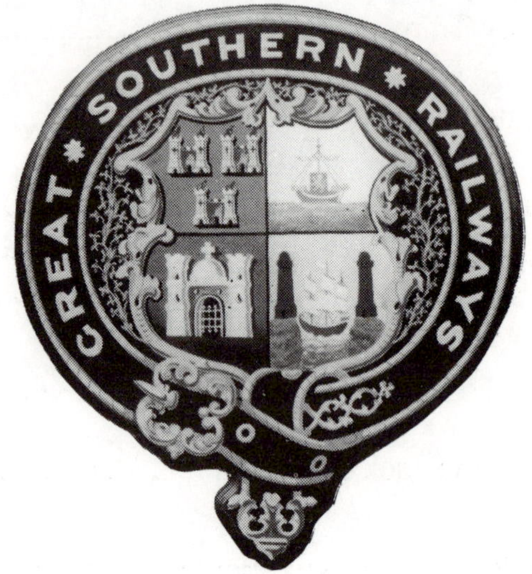
GREAT * SOUTHERN * RAILWAYS

The job and life in a different era

My railway career began when I joined the Great Southern Railway (G. S. R.) on the 19th January 1936.

It was a private company which comprised of seven directors and controlled by a general manager, traffic manager and secretary. I did not realise it at the time, but I was to be a railwayman for nearly fifty years, half a century of people and transport, just like my father before me.

He worked as a shunter and capstan for forty years and remembers how my present house on Summerhill, over-looking the railway, was occupied by British army officers during the wars years. He worked through the Civil War in 1922 and like me, saw a lot of changes in the patterns of social life of Ireland. He retired in 1969.

One of the conditions of my employment, when I joined the Great Southern Railway in 1936, was that I pass a medical examination which took place at Kingsbridge Station in Dublin, now known as Heuston Station. I was stripped down and given two watches and asked which of the two was ticking – that was the hearing test. Next came the tests for sight and colour

The Man from the Railway

blindness: I was asked to read from a board with letters on it and to read out a sign across the road from the station. I then had to identify the colours of a set of ribbons. I proved medically sound and presented myself to the Stationmaster in Cork.

On my first day I was given a rule book and a measurement form to be provided with a corduroy uniform at a later stage. My wages at the time as a Junior Porter were 15s.9d. I was on my way to being The Man from the Railway.

The Man from the Railway

Staff travel facilities were generous. Each employee was entitled to six free passes and privilege concession tickets for cross channel and European travel. Misuse of such benefits was frowned upon. I recall a case where a member of staff unwittingly lent his free pass to a relative and when challenged said that he had put his ticket in his shaving gear case for safety. When his friend required to shave the temptation overcame common sense and he took the pass. The staff member was given the benefit of the doubt and was pardoned.

It was essential that employees of the company join a trade union. Staff were represented by a member elected to discuss with management staff problems such as duty rosters, uniforms, entitlements and disciplinary procedures. A breach of the rules was conveyed to the offending party on a charge sheet by the District Superintendent and a date for the hearing arranged and attended by trade union officials. We mostly felt it was a just system.

My first turn of duty was from 12.30 p.m. to 9.30 p.m. and this involved washing carriages in the carriage sheds where the various trains were stabled. This was adjacent to the new car park which was the original loading bay, opposite the Arcadia Ballroom. As I was the rookie (the new recruit) I found myself doing most of the adult work. I spent nearly all of my time in the carriage sheds sweeping and mopping out the coaches.

The Man from the Railway

This task was a tedious one. Most of the rolling stock comprised of box carriages which had separate compartments, some marked 'Ladies'. Even then the fair sex was catered for.

Relics of old decency with the Great Southern Railway

The cleaning of the trains was of great importance. Door handles were brassed and destination boards, which were fitted on the roof of main line trains, were taken down and washed. During the summer months the exterior of the trains was dry cleaned by a substance called *waste* made up of cotton and thread material. The dirt was mainly loose dust so it was quite easy to get off with regular cleaning..

The Man from the Railway

The compartments of the trains were quite well decorated at the time. Most of them had calico curtains and plush velvet seats with beautiful picture views of Ireland in colour by Lawrence.

The seats were kept clean by using a portable vacuum cleaner known as **The Bug Chaser**. Prior to vacuuming, the seats were beaten with a rubber hose to bring the dust to the surface, as well as some of the non-paying customers. The presence of the fleas would be revealed by the occasional mark on the shirt collar as well as an unpleasant itch. As you can imagine it was a job to be avoided.

The Doctor's Job was so called because whoever had it was responsible for the sparkling white linen for the waiting room and the train hand towels, which were of white linen with a red band bordering the edges. Everything was white, just like a doctor's coat. The Doctor was also in charge of changing the white antimacassars for the first class carriages. Bars of soap were also supplied by him. The linens were cleaned by the Metropole Laundry which was situated opposite St. Patrick's Church. The chimney stack of the laundry graced the Cork skyline until it was demolished when the laundry closed down in the sixties.

The Trimmer, as he was known, was employed in sewing the cushions and fabric of the train seats. This was done regularly, and any report of a missing trim or open seam was immediately attended to.

The Man from the Railway

The Bug Chaser

The Man from the Railway

Train examiners were a special class of employee who were skilled in examining the general conditions of carriages. Tapping the wheels with a hammer, they determined whether or not the axle boxes were overheating or if the wheel tyre was slack. Carriages which were found unsuitable on a train were detached and put into a siding, marked with a NOT TO GO red label attached to the running board and it was considered a criminal offense to remove them.

In the early days it was possible to order a tea basket from the hotel at the price of 3s.6d., to take on the train. The baskets were collected at Limerick Junction. Here, there was a full sized bar and refreshment room. This offered a welcome repast for travellers and the railway crew alike and boiling water for the billy can was obtainable to make the cuppa tea.

Foot-warmers were also available for first class travellers .

It was a time when the availability of money certainly made travel much more comfortable.

The waiting rooms in the early days were not attractive places. The walls were painted green, adorned with a large sized framed map of the railway system, with a few photographs of Irish scenery. The seats were wooden slatted. A porter entered when it

The Man from the Railway

was necessary to announce the arrival of incoming trains and inform the travellers when the check barrier was open for departing trains. This is done now by announcements on the public address system. Waiting room attendants were employed to supervise as well as female cleaners to keep the place ship shape.

The Cork station in its present state has changed almost completely, most of the offices have been replaced by new and more modern ones. The buffet still remains unchanged in its exterior, facing the station yard and when controlled by the Great Southern Railway was a full hotel in which the travellers stayed.

The various hotels had representatives attending at the station to collect passengers who were booked with them. I remember the Metropole Hotel had a float drawn by a powerful looking horse which featured in a book written about it entitled 'Amber Eyes'. The driver was a man named Paddy. Con, who represented Paddy Cook's Travel Agents wore a pill box shaped cap, similar to the French Gendarmerie, with Cooks inscribed in Gold letters on it. He was known as The Man from Cooks.

The Man from the Railway

As time went by I entertained thoughts of quitting because of the late duty. At the age of sixteen I felt I was missing out on a lot -playing football in the evening with friends, going cycling and dancing. I was going from bed to work. Eventually, I succeeded in getting an early turn of duty, 9.30 a.m. to 6.00 p.m., which brought me on to platform duties.

As a general porter, I was assigned various duties from sweeping the platforms to carrying passengers' luggage to and from the trains. At that time the carrying of luggage could be a financial bonus, depending on the type of passenger one met. The minimum tip was a sixpenny bit and, if one were lucky to meet a more well-off passenger, the chances of a half crown were in the offing and this would put you over the moon.

In those days I could buy thirty squares of Urney's chocolate or a bottle of lemonade for 2d., a packet of biscuits for 4d. or dance the night away at the Arcadia for 1s.6d. to Mick Delahunty and other local bands. They playing mainly céilí music and old tyme waltzes – none of that tango and rumba business –they were all strange to us.

I went to dancing classes and eventually graduated from the Gresham Rooms in Maylor Street on 19th May 1942. My first visit there was torture as I didn't want to go there in the first place. It was my brother who encouraged me, in fact it was through losing the

The Man from the Railway

toss of a coin that I got there at all. It was like going to the scaffold as I was the shy type. I couldn't pluck up the courage to ask a girl to dance and it was not until I was asked up on to the floor for a lady's choice that I ventured forth. I warned the young lady that I was a *legger* , and that I was likely to step on her toes, but she took a chance. Of course the dancing was quite difficult to get the hang of - the military two-step, the Viennese Waltz and the Barn Dance all took time to learn. There was none of today's close dancing or wild flinging around of legs and arms - everything was controlled and organised. My luck was in and I survived and had to admit to both my partner that night and my brother that I even enjoyed it a little. Tea and cakes were served by Thompsons bakery during the intermission, so the whole evening was really very pleasant. I ended up going dancing most nights. All work and no play does no man any good.

The Man from the Railway

In many ways what we lacked in cash was made up in kind. There was the early morning train from Mallow, which carried a few churns of fresh cream for a well known dairy in Shandon Street. Their ice cream was *par excellence*. and a few drops of cream would often enliven a railwayman's tea. Then we had the rabbits, which came in crates and a stray one might put meat in a stew pot. The fish from broken boxes often made a savoury fry in a railwayman's pan, as well as the travelling fowl who had their eggs collected by members of staff.

The parcel office was also a great scene of activity because all goods such as parcels, cartons and other miscellaneous items had to be brought to the counter and, depending on the nature of the goods offered for transport, had to be stamped, weighed and, in most cases, a consignment note completed. There were the different brands of butter: Black Swan, (Dowdall O'Mahony) C&K (Cork and Kerry) and of course the cartons of confectionery from Thompsons Bakery, along with large hampers of bread for the various shopkeepers who were customers of the firm. Sometimes there was an auction of slightly damaged confectionery which hadn't fared too well in the course of transport.

Yeast was a commodity which, because of its composition, had to be handled with care. It was placed in jute bags and contained in green rush woven

The Man from the Railway

baskets. The Cork Yeast Company, which had its headquarters on the Watercourse Road, supplied yeast as far away as Lifford in Co. Donegal. Their biggest customer at the time was Messrs. Haughton on Ormond Quay in Dublin. The yeast was dispatched in a wagon on the night mail.

Unloading the night mail train

As time went by I was exposed to more of the workings of the railway.

Each train was equipped with a tail lamp attached to the last coach to ensure that the train was complete. I was detailed to sign for tail lamps of all main line trains on arrival. This I did at the Central Cabin, as it

The Man from the Railway

was then known. I spent a week learning the workings of the signal cabin and was fascinated with the various levers which controlled the movement of the trains and shunting operations in the passenger area and goods yard. A large diagram board displayed the progress of the trains which entered the tunnel from both ends. A noisy repeating indicator signalled the approach of trains from Cobh and Youghal after passing Myrtlehill gate crossing, which is still in existence.

Train lighting was supplied in most carriages by gas delivered from Limerick and was contained in cylindrical tanks and positioned at the side of the carriage shed. Gas cocks were fitted between the mainline up and down tracks whilst the Cobh and Youghal trains were gassed from the bays. The lamp room, which contained the oil for the train tail-lamps and signal cases, was controlled by one of the lamp-men who was very exact in ensuring that the lamps were cleaned and the wicks pared to ensure that they functioned. Sometimes the tail-lamps would blow out during the course of a journey. When this irregularity occurred, the train was stopped at the next station and the defective lamp was lit.

One of the porters on the 12.30 p.m. duty was detailed to take six signal lamp cases with him as far as Tivoli Bridge. These lit the signals and level crossing lamps on that section of the line. Many curses were uttered on a breezy day when nearly half a box of matches

The Man from the Railway

would be used in trying to light the lamps for the Tivoli Bridge signals.

Cobh

October 1954, Cobh station. Arrival of tender and passengers from liner

I spent three years working at Cobh Station and at that time Cobh was a booming town. Often, special trains would be laid on as three passenger liners could arrive in the one day. The American mailbags were stacked at the departure platform and the big trunks which the emigrants brought were often compared to small labourers' cottages.

There was also a customs post at the station to deal with incoming and outgoing passengers to America. All outgoing trunks were weighed here and charges levied for extra weight. These charges were often paid

The Man from the Railway

in dollars so the clerk would have to know the exchange rate. The steel workers from Cork City arrived here, as did passengers travelling from Cork to places in the west of Ireland, like Galway and Ballinasloe. They would all require different tickets and would have to change trains at Limerick Junction or Portarlington, depending on their destination. The station was a hive of activity.

Hotels like the States Hotel (now the Commodore) and

President and Mrs Eisenhower at Cobh Station after their arrivial from the U.S.A.

the Westbourne were open all the year round and did a roaring trade. On Sundays you could see the ladies sitting on benches along the front.

I had the pleasure of meeting the famous Mayo soprano, Margaret Burke Sheridan. She was a well

The Man from the Railway

built, well fed woman, as they say, and she wore a big wide brimmed hat and a white fur around her collar. I got her autograph. She wasn't too willing at first as she said she had a train to catch. However, when I told her I was going to be on the train she quickly agreed. I also met Cardinal Cushing, a very stately man, not unlike Cardinal Hume of Westminster. He was tall and commanding with a slow and dignified walk. I doffed

Relatives waiting to greet homecoming emigrants

my cap and welcomed him to Ireland and asked him for his autograph."Certainly", he said, "but it won't get you into heaven."

The paddle steamer Albert, owned by Cork, Blackrock & Passage Railway, pictured off Cuskinny, Cobh

Youghal

No book on Irish railways would be complete without reference to Youghal. Many generations of Cork people travelled there every Sunday to indulge in a relaxing day at the seaside, or avail of the Sea Breeze excursions on Wednesday at 2.30 p.m., the fare being 1s.6d.

A day on the strand at Youghal

One Sunday, with the rest of the porters, I went to Youghal to sweep out the carriages which was a thirsty and tiring job. I was invited by my work-mate to a licensed premises across the road from the station for refreshments, my drink was a mineral. We were

The Man from the Railway

upbraided by the Station Master at the time who reported us to the District Superintendent and he admonished my senior colleague for showing me bad example at the start of my railway career. Our spokesman at the meeting with the Superintendent was

Youghal Station.

a character known as 'Mutt'. At the 'trial' he remarked "the engine which hauled the train to Youghal had to be watered", just as we had to be. We got off with a caution.

It has to be said that the staff members were very loyal to each other and there was always the great 'cover up' for staff absent during working hours for various reasons from football matches to race meetings to visits to certain licensed premises to quench a thirst.

The Man from the Railway

With the closure of the Youghal line, **Fenit,** which is about six miles from Tralee station, became the Mecca for Cork people to enjoy a day at the sea side. I remember one particular Sunday when a youngster, anxious to board the train at Tralee, was restrained by his aunt because he was a mischievous young man and she didn't want to let him out of her jurisdiction. However, he managed to get on the train and when he saw me during the course of my train checking he disappeared from view. I was concerned about this because I wondered if he had jumped out of the train, which was slow moving on this section of the line. It transpired that his buddies had put him under the seat in their carriage compartment. On the return trip I made him clean himself, as his clothes and hands were dirty from being under the seat. He was handed over to his aunt who had guessed what had happened and gave him a good cuffing.

Fenit, July 1959.

The Man from the Railway

Bridge Street, Tralee, 31 March 1961

The Man from the Railway

The Cork and Muskerry Light Railway, or **the Blarney Tram** as it was known, had its headquarters on the Western Road on the site now occupied by Jury's Hotel. All that remains of the bridge, spanning the South Channel of the river Lee, are the piers.

1915: A locomotive of the Cork & Muskerry Light railway and an electric tram meet on Western Road.

The timetable during the forties was as follows:-

Weekdays:
Western Road Departure: 8 a.m. 10a.m. 1p.m. 3p.m. 5p.m. 7p.m.
Blarney Departure: 9a.m. 11a.m. 2p.m. 4p.m. 6p.m. 8p.m.
FARES: First Class 1s.8d : Third Class 10d.

The route served was: Cork, Victoria Cross, Carrigrohane, Leemount Halt, Healy's Bridge, Coachford Junction, Cloghroe, Gurteen Halt, Dripsey, Kilmurry, Ballast Pit, Coachford, Coachford Junction, Tower Bridge Halt, St. Annes, Donoughmore Junction, Blarney.

The Man from the Railway

As time progressed requests were made by the increasing population around Gaol Cross to have the tram stopped. This was eventually agreed to, though not in the early stages of the tram's operation. Fares from Gaol Cross were 2d. single first class, and 1d. third class single. It was amusing to race with the tram on a bicycle and, more times than not, the cyclist would pass it out. The Cork Tramway could be seen with one of the trams travelling beside the train. I suppose these could be classified as "friendly" transport rivals.

On the 6th May 1893 the **Donoughmore** Branch opened to the public. The first train leaving the terminus at 7 a.m., the opposite working tram Cork departing at 8.15 a.m. It was a lovely journey out to the countryside. Donoughmore parish was partly in the barony of Barrett's, chiefly in East Muskerry east Riding and some of the tributaries of the Lee and Blackwater have their rise in the district.

Train services were as follows:
Weekdays
Donoughmore Departure 7a.m., 10.30a.m., 4.30p.m.
Western Road Departure 8.15 a.m. 2 p.m. 4.30p.m.
Sunday
Donoughmore Departure: 10a.m. 12.15p.m. 4.30p.m.
Western Road Departure: 10a.m. 12.15p.m. 6p.m.
FARES - CORK - DONOUGHMORE
Single First Class 1s.8d - Third Class 1s.1d.
Return First Class 2/6d - Third Class 1s.6d.

The Ticket Collector

Ticket collectors had to be careful when performing their duties.
When a collector finished checking tickets in one carriage he had to go outside that carriage to get into the next one. This was done while the train was moving. The doors were at the ends of the coaches and opened in so he pulled the door after him as he went out. He supported himself by hanging onto the iron bars attached to the coach and standing on the narrow steps, just outside the door. He then swung himself onto the next coach, supporting himself the same way, pushed the door in, and proceeded with his work in that coach. The whole performance was dangerous, especially on a wet day, as the outside steps were wet and slippery. Anyone who is familiar with the Tarzan films, starring Johnny Weissmuller, might agree with me that if a stunt man was necessary for the actor, they could do worse than approach one of the ticket collectors on these lines. The agility required to perform their ticket collecting duties surely qualified them.

When I was promoted to Travelling Ticket Collector I really got an insight into human nature. The toilets on train were a haven for those who tried to avoid paying their fare. After a period of working on the trains the ticket collectors would adopt their own method of

The Man from the Railway

beating the rogue system. I used to use a bit of cunning, knocking on the toilet door and then pretending to walk away, giving the impression to the occupant that I had gone. Actually I would be standing a few feet away from the door. In most cases the person concerned would pay up.

Excursion trains, especially match specials, produced the most interesting scams. It was not unusual to find more than one person travelling on one ticket. The ticket would be pushed under the toilet door when the checker knocked and called out 'tickets please'. But this hoax was defeated because it was possible to open the toilet door from the outside by turning the engaged sign to vacant. This was easy to do because it was a rotary disc. The villains would be caught red handed. Problems were also caused on excursion trains by the rowdy attitude of drunken passengers who sometimes pulled the communication cord, causing the train to stop. This meant that the guard and checker on the train would have to go through the train to find out in which carriage the chain was pulled, but seldom were the perpetrators caught. The fine at the time was £5.

The job of ticket collector involved a bit more than checking tickets. Half an hour before departure I inspected all the compartments. I had to check to see that the toilets flushed properly and that there were clean towels and soaps etc. The seating, lighting and reservation of seats were also my responsibility and I had to report anything out of order on a special report

The Man from the Railway

sheet which was handed in at the terminus so it could be fixed before next departure. Standards were very high and nothing was ever left out of order for more than twenty-four hours. We had some particularly fussy directors who would check under the seats for debris and, if any was found, a report would be sent to the station master. The cleaning staff would be severely reprimanded if their work was not up to scratch. While it might have seemed strict for us at the time the system worked very well and it was a pleasure to be part of such an efficient organisation.

The Crash of '27

The railway made headline news when a collision between a tram and a steam roller occurred on the 6th September 1927 at Inchigaggin, half way between

Carrigrohane and Victoria Cross. The 1.15 p.m. from Blarney hauled by engine No. 8K was travelling at a moderate speed along the roadside when the steamroller working on road repairs ran into the tram, damaging the engine and derailing two bogie coaches. One of them is believed to have been thrown into a nearby field. The passengers were brought out through the windows of the carriages and there was much excitement, but no serious injuries. The impact

The Man from the Railway

dislodged the front roller of the road machine from its bearings. The train engine was able to continue to Cork and the line was re-opened the following day.

Looking back at the old stations

Other railways which were in operation at the time were Cork to Macroom, Cork to Blackrock and

Crosshaven Station in the early 30s

Cork to Crosshaven. With the advent of the buses these and the Cork to Muskerry, (sometimes called "The Hook and Eye"), ceased to exist. On the 29th day of December 1934, the last train left Cork for Blarney.

Today very little remains of the buildings which were part of the Muskerry line. The best preserved building is the Blarney Station, painted white and now serving as a public convenience for both sexes, whilst a railway shed at the rear is now a shop. The station yards, since covered with tarmac', provide considerable parking space for cars and touring buses.

The Man from the Railway

"Paddy" draws a wagon from Shannon Vale up to the main line in Clonakilty.

Loco No. 156, Newmarket, June 1959

The Man from the Railway

"The Peake" at Blarney Station, 1933

Mitchelstown Station.

The Man from the Railway

Kanturk, 1959

The last day of Macroom Railway. Macroom Station, November 1953

The Man from the Railway

Christmas was a very busy time in the Parcels Office and I was often drafted in to assist in the stamping of the various consignments. One incident which I must mention was the substitution of a Kerry Blue terrier captured on the Lower Glanmire Road for a pedigree dog which escaped when the door to the Parcels Office was left open. The substitute was then consigned to a retired English military officer in Staffordshire, festooned with address labels and instructions for feeding and watering. A stipend of £2.00 was given to the guard on the Rosslare train in which the dog travelled. No more was ever heard of the substitute. I wonder what was the outcome. If the officer knew his dogs it may well have been a case of 'Military Man bites Dog'.

Saturday was also a busy day on the load bank from 9a.m. to 1p.m. because a special shipping train to Rosslare Harbour left at 1.30p.m. With it went wagons containing frozen rabbits, salmon, plucks in casks and veal hanging from bars six inches apart to keep from swinging or touching during the course of the journey.

Rosslare Harbour was one of the places I liked staying overnight, especially in the summertime. It was lovely in the morning. My memory is of myself and the train guard walking down the hill from the dormitory to the station and the vision of the blue sky reflected in the calm ocean. The wisps of smoke from a ship in the distance, heralded the arrival of the passenger boat

The Man from the Railway

from Fishguard Harbour. The hundreds of passengers on board were comprised mostly of holiday makers who would be travelling on the 6.15 a.m. express train to Cork. I would be on duty at 5.30 a.m. to check the tickets of the passengers on to the waiting train when they cleared customs.

When the train moved off after leaving Fermoy, most of the passengers would have alighted and I looked forward to a savoury breakfast supplied by Denis who was the head waiter in the dining car. However, my taste buds were sometimes disappointed due to signalling regulations. I would have to travel on the engine with the short staff, an instrument which protected the single line from another train entering the section and causing a collision. This exercise was brought into action when usually a goods train was stopped at Castletownroche or Ballyhooley, which were halts on the Fermoy/Mallow section.

Joe, Jimmy and Jack

The demise of Joe Loss, the famous band-leader, recalls my trip to Dublin on a special train. As we were staying overnight, the guard and myself decided to see the Joe Loss Show at the Theatre Royal. The cost was 7s.6d. for the dress circle. Like the old Opera House in Cork the dress circle of the Theatre Royal was very plush with red velvet seats and boxes for the upper classes. The guard and I were attired in our corduroy uniforms and, on ascending the stairs of the dress circle, two attendants closed in on us, thinking that we were gate crashers. We stood out like sore thumbs, of course, as every other man was in a dress suit. However, on producing our tickets we were shown to our seats. It was the first time Joe Loss had toured Ireland. The show also included Ruby Murray and the Alice Delgarno dancing girls. It was Joe Loss who set Ruby Murray on the road to fame with her song "My Sweet Dublin Bay". It was a fantastic, glamourous night - even if we did stick out like two signal lights.

The Man from the Railway
JIMMY O'DEA AND JACK CRUISE

Many of the big theatrical companies played at the old Cork Opera house. None were more popular with railwaymen than Jimmy O'Dea and his entourage because those who unloaded the stage props and scenery were given free tickets for his show. Other famous theatrical names of the day were Jack Cruise and Carl Clopet. The sets for the Carl Clopet Company were big and cumbersome and had to be handled carefully when unloading as the paint could come off or small bits jutting off could be broken. All the costumes came from Gings packed in big wicker skips. The arrival of a theatre company always caused a stir as there was something magical and flamboyant about the people who travelled with them.

The Specials

Mystery trains were a popular mid week activity. On one occasion, when a porter was delegated to inform intending passengers that the train was going to Killarney, it resulted in a queue at the ticket office because most of the intending passengers had been there before and wanted a refund.

Knock Pilgrimage Specials were an edifying experience for me. The fortitude of the invalids and sick people who travelled in a special ambulance coach made me realise how lucky I was to enjoy good health. Tribute must be paid to the devoted West Cork people who travelled in the early hours of the morning to join the main pilgrimage trains from Cork to Knock. The closure of the West Cork railway was a big blow to the community there, as well as to the city people who travelled on the 9.a.m. train on Sunday mornings. This train left from Albert Quay and served Clonakilty providing access to Inchadoney Strand and the terminus at Courtmacsherry. The closing of the railway marked the end of an era.

Special excursion trains were a feature of the rail promotions programme but the showpiece of them all was the International Radio Train which ran three times a week from Dublin to Killarney with a radio studio and compere. It broadcast throughout the train. The passengers were encouraged to join in the

The Man from the Railway

broadcast and sing along with the music. Full catering services of a high standard were provided. The compere would give some of the local history and anecdotes. I remember when we were passing through Limerick Junction we were told about one of the Galtee mountains. It was known as The Devil's Bit. It was said that the devil in a rage took a bite out of the mountains and spit it out in the sea which formed the Isle of Man. When we stopped at Mallow he told us about the mineral springs which were plentiful in Ireland during the 18th and 19th century.

Now that I look back I believe it is to be regretted that their promotion as a tourist attraction has not been contemplated, especially the spa at Mallow which was well known at one time. In fact Mallow's spa was considered to be on a par with Bath in England.

The radio compere was good at relating stories of the questionable characters in Mallow, what we would term Chancers. They enjoyed all sorts of shady transactions. There was a lot of heavy drinking and gambling going on in those days which often resulted in arguments and street brawls. It was these characters who inspired the composition of the famous ballad 'The Rakes of Mallow':

> "Then to this raking life
> They got sober, take a wife,
> Ever after live in strife
> And wish again for Mallow".

The Man from the Railway

Leaving for Kerry with the Sam Maguire Cup

The paper train from Dublin, which arrived in the early hours of the morning, was an important one

The County Board including Seán Óg Murphy and Pádraig O'Keeffe (Parc Uí Chaoimh was named after him)

The Man from the Railway

because all the national daily papers were brought here to be collected by the various news-agents at the station. The staff involved in sorting out same were rewarded with a free copy.

Most of the Head Offices in Dublin were supplied with a copy of the Cork Examiner which was dispatched on the 7.45 a.m. train. I remember being dismayed when I observed a guard on the train, who was a racing enthusiast, separating the racing pages from the paper and putting the rest back in the wrapper. I reminded him that he was doing wrong and would be detected but he replied 'those guys weren't interested in racing and wouldn't cop it anyway'. He was probably right.

Press letters were an important item sent by train to the various publications. I recall that on one Sunday, when I was stationed in Cobh, a very important yacht race was in progress and the result was to be sent to the Cork Examiner office in town for publication. However, the porter forgot to send the result in by train and was horrified when he discovered his error. He offered me all the tea in China to get the result to the Examiner office as quickly as possible. By the time I arrived at 'De Paper' it was midnight. I succeeded in getting in by a door up a side lane off Patrick Street, just before the presses started to roll. My colleague breathed a deep sight of relief when he saw the result published in the Monday morning edition.

The Man from the Railway

The night mail train departed at about 8.45 p.m. and also had a passenger coach. It arrived in Dublin at 3.a.m. The mail was brought to the station in a box-shaped green van marked P&T in gold lettering and drawn by two horses. The mail train was a gleaming spectacle of steel coaches which were dark red in colour with a black stripe under the windows which were of glistening chromium with matching door handles. This being an express train, the mail was gathered en route at non-stop stations by a net attached to the travelling post office in front of the train which snatched the mailbags from a column at the end of the platform. This, as you can imagine, called for skillful manoeuvring. The mail was conveyed in the travelling post office at the front of the train, while the mail for Limerick and Waterford was put in a sealed wagon. This was detached at Limerick Junction where the train arrived at midnight. The rear portion of the train went on directly to Dun Laoighre to connect with the Hollyhead boat.

The incoming night mail train provided a busy few hours for the staff on duty. I was always interested in gaining access into motor van 86M which contained the films for Cobh, Youghal and West Cork as well as the local cinemas in Cork City, the Savoy, The Washington, Pavillion, Lee Cinema, Assembly Rooms and the Coliseum, all of which are now part of Cork's cinema history. I was interested in the outside labels giving the names of the stars, Gene Autrey, Tom Mix and the studio names like Columbia, M.G.M.,

The Man from the Railway

Paramount and of course Louis Elliman. Like the theatrical companies, the incoming film reels brought magic into my life, a little bit of make-believe.

The movement of cattle from various fairs and cattle marts to Roscrea and the North Wall in Dublin was a big event at the station. This was controlled by a District Inspector with loading staff as well as the buyers and exporters who attended and paid for the number of wagons they required for their stock. Regulations permitted only a certain number of beasts in each wagon, but telling tales out of school, an extra beast would be slipped in, thus avoiding the cost of an extra wagon. This was all accomplished with a nod and a wink -and a small backhander for the loader.

The transport of livestock from Bantry and Bandon cattle fairs was a regular occurrence across the twin bridges, Clontarf and Brian Boru, and through the cutting opposite St. Patrick's Church. Each train was preceded by a flagman carrying a red flag, the train, of course, proceeding at a snail's pace.

A feature of the Brian Boru bridge was that it was under the control of the railway and opened upwards on both sides to allow mostly coal-boats to pass through. Most of the coal used by the railway came from Belfast in the familiar Kelly coal-boats with their red, white and blue funnels. One of these was the Clew Bay which had a siren with a sound like a banshee. These boats docked on Horgan's Quay, and

The Man from the Railway

wagons for unloading emerged from the goods yard on to the quay-side. The railway tracks are still visible.

Brian Boru Bridge, 1911, showing the tracks of Bandon Railway which crossed the bridge to Cork Station.

The War Years

The Second World War, or The Emergency as it was known in Ireland, brought some changes to the Cork station. The glass roof of the station was blacked out and trains were fitted with black curtains. The edge of the platforms were painted white to ensure the safety of the passengers getting on and off the trains and two air raid shelters were provided in the station yard.

During The Emergency most of the army were stationed at Rockgrove, served by Little Island station. The last train to Cobh was often boisterous because of the conflict between soldiers and sailors, the latter being from a British mine-sweeper unit attached to Cobh. This train was always met by military policemen known as 'Redcaps' in case of complaint by the train crew.

The war years taught people to be resourceful. I have always had a sweet tooth and at that time sugar was scarce, so I used boiled sweets to sweeten my tea by dropping them into the billycan of hot water and stirring them until they melted. The sound of them falling into the can often drew the comment from staff members to the effect that 'Mac' was dropping his bombs again. However, they did the job and I got my dose of sweetness.

The Man from the Railway

Keeping warm was another problem which had to be reckoned with due to the restricted supply of fuel for household and industrial purposes. Being on duty from midnight to 9.a.m. was often a chilling experience during the war. My mate and I depended on the kindness of the fireman on the last train from Cobh, who would give us a bucket of coal, which we secretly deposited in the carriage shed. After a time we noticed that our supply was fast disappearing so we decided that we would have to investigate. We lay in wait in a dark carriage in an attempt to catch the thief red-handed. We did this by filling a small bag with stones and putting a few lumps of coal at the top of the bag, giving the impression that it was full of coal. Our plan was rewarded when the culprit, who lived near the railway, came along and hoisted the bag onto his shoulder. He went down the path outside the carriage shed and lobbed the bag over the wall of his yard. It didn't happen again, a case of the 'bitter bitten'.

The fuel shortage during the emergency meant that the steam locomotives were run on turf processed into briquettes at Inchicore in Dublin. Most of the branch lines had their sleepers broken up for fuel. This whole procedure recalled to mind the line from that song by Percy French about the West Clare Railway, 'do you think that we'll be there before the night'. Mind you, strange fuel or no, the trains always arrived.

Engines on the line

The St. Maloga was the small engine which functioned on the West Cork Railways and was named after the saint who is associated with Timoleague Abbey (Tig Molaga).

The Macha

The Macha (Loco 801). The strange suggestion concerning Macha was that she outran the chariot horses of the well known King of Ulster, Conor Mac Nessa, a product of Irish mythology who incurred the wrath of the king's household. Thus the reference to the speed of the loco Macha. This was one of the 800 class engines which hauled the Cork-Dublin express passenger trains before the introduction of diesel locomotives on the rail system.

The Man from the Railway

Co. Waterford viaduct beyond Dungarvan.

Glenesk viaduct.

Kilnap, 1950.

The Man from the Railway

Locomotive No.171, Slieve Gullion

Near Glenbeigh, 1953

En route to Crosshaven.

Great Southern Railcar, Newmarket 1928.

Characters and Anecdotes

The stationmaster in Cork was known as **The Rajah**: He walked in a military way with his hands held behind his back. In his long black frock-coat, railway cap with embroidered crest, white shirt and red tie, he bore an uncanny resemblance to General De Gaulle. I wasn't scared of him, but, as he was the boss, you did not want to incur his displeasure. He had the power to suspend you for a week or demote you. I never remember anyone being sacked, however, some were put on suspension. The suspensions were incurred mainly for the crime of 'missing from duty' and those involved were, on most occasions, to be found in the pub across the road. The true reason, of course, would never be put on the charge sheet, the Form A, as it was up to the staff member to make up the best lie possible. The Rajah was very tolerant of people like myself; as a new boy I was excused on a few occasions on the grounds that it was my first time making a mistake. All in all, so long as the work was done there was no problem.

The Man from the Railway

Con the Foreman

He was a genial individual of advanced years. There was a story about him to the effect that he would have been shot by the Black and Tans but was spared because of his age.

He was about sixty and looked it. He had a round red face and had a carefree attitude to life. He would say to me "young fella, go out there and make some money for yourself". In the early days, when I was a greenhorn, I would get left behind while the other fellows were out *tacking* –getting passengers. They would run to a carriage and catch the door handle which meant that any tips for the carrying of luggage was theirs. I was always in the carriage shed sweeping and doing the donkey work while the rest were out tacking. It was Con who put me wise. Once I understood the drill I would sprint out and soon built up speed to beat some of them to the mark. I would bring the passengers' luggage onto the train, fix it in the rack, doff my cap, and the money would be handed over. Most people were very decent, but there was one character who belonged to a Cork drapery firm and regularly travelled with two big skips which were very heavy. In fact they were always overweight, but he didn't care as the firm paid for the excess baggage. We would have to load them and after all our work we were lucky to get a sixpence. (He had to pay the tip out of his own money). When we got to know him we would all disappear when we saw him arriving, and he would report that there were no porters to be seen. Eventually we devised a system whereby we would be visible when he arrived, but gone when he needed us.

The Man from the Railway

Mossy

Listowel races were a very important fixture in the South. One year I was on checking duty between Tralee and Listowel, accompanied by an Inspector and two Dublin Checkers. One of them was called Mossy. He dressed very tastefully and had a very dignified manner. His colleague would provoke a storm in heaven just for the fun of it. We were strolling down the street on one occasion with the aforementioned colleague when he spotted Mossy sitting on a bar stool, having a drink. He shouted at Mossy to the effect that he should be ashamed of himself indulging himself when he had a wife and six children in poor circumstances at home. Our accommodation that night was a sleeping car with bunk beds and restricted space. Things got hot and heavy when a row broke out between `Mossy' and his buddy over the remark. The Inspector and myself had to intervene to prevent blows being struck.

Later, we got a scare when the Inspector became ill as a result of food poisoning. He recovered when I gave him a sedative to ease his pain. The next morning our fun loving friend told the inspector that he had lit a candle for him as he thought he was dying and that he had already sent in an application for his job. It takes all kinds.

The loading of the night mail was directed by one of the porters known as **Gordon Richards** because of his diminutive stature. Gordon Richards was the smallest

The Man from the Railway

jockey in England and he was knighted. He was said to have been 'the shortest knight'. Our Gordon Richards was very tense, as a jockey would be before a race, and as light as a fairy with black hair receding. H e was a familiar face to many who used the railway in those days.

Jimmy , the porter, was known as **Pusheen** because he loved the cats that hung around the railway station waiting for the pigeons who came for the grain. He used to stroke them gently and call them all Pusheen. At the time we transported a lot of ferrets. They came from England for the Stoker family. They were used for hunting rabbits. They would arrive in slatted boxes and we would have to be careful that our fingers did not come in contact with them as they would be quickly bitten off. I remember when a box load of ferrets broke loose and invaded the station. The place was over-run with them. The staff ran away from, rather than after them, as they were afraid a ferret might go up the legs of their trousers. Pusheen came to the rescue. He was very fit, as he ran with the hunt, and went beagling. He ran after each ferret in beagle fashion, almost sniffing them out. He caught each one by the back of the neck and returned the marauders to their box. Pusheen was the hero of the day.

The Man from the Railway

The person who dealt with the weighing of luggage was known as **The Holy Father**, because he was regarded as a decent living man and never failed to recite the Angelus irrespective of what was happening around him. He was a keen supporter of the Riverstown Harriers Beagle Club.

Padna was a character who used give me his corduroy uniform to pawn on my way home and the 15s. advanced on it was usually spent on drink. When his daughter was about to make her First Holy Communion the Stationmaster at the time fitted her out.

Danny Gilpin was small and wiry like a leprechaun, hot tempered and quick to take offense. Dark haired, sallow complexioned with aquiline features, he wore a uniform of jacket, pants, blue shirt and red tie. It was hard to know the colour of Danny's shirt as it got dirty from his work. He was dedicated to his job and could not understand anyone doing anything wrong or anything on the job going wrong. He buzzed around very quickly.

The Lamb was pale faced, of slender build and average height. He seemed very nice on first meeting but you found out very quickly that he faulted everything. I would say 'its a fine morning' and he would reply 'what's fine about it?' He was a terrible man for money and would push you aside when the trains arrived to get to the passengers first. Once I got 7s.6d. from a passenger, which was a huge amount. He was very disgruntled and asked me how I managed it. 'Courtesy' I replied. It was something that The Lamb was not acquainted with at all.

On one occasion I remember the Chief Clerk in the Parcels Office replying to a 'smart alec' that he called his dog Knickerbocker because the dog's breath came in short pants.

Then there was **Tuppence** who was always short that amount to purchase a packet of cigarettes.

Forty Tanners was the one who criticised those who purchased raffle tickets, bet on horses or indulged in the odd pint as being foolish because if they saved their 'tanners' they would have a few pounds to their credit. He used to say that most of the licensed premises across the road from the station were painted by railwaymen's money.

The Chink or Chinaman was an individual with sallow complexion and close knit eyes. Whenever he was in bad humour it was reckoned that he had not had his rice that day

The Man from the Railway

Dali Lama was a very religious man who was a porter. He would sit crossed-legged with his arms folded. He was tall with curly hair which was thin on top but came down over his eyes untidily like the hair of a Kerry Blue. He would always bless himself if he received anything resembling bad news.

A Rookie : On the first day on the job a new man would be sent to the Stationmaster's office to get the keys of the tunnel gates which of course were non-existent.

Tom Semple: I had the pleasure of meeting the man after whom Semple Stadium is named as he was a guard on the 5.10 p.m. train from Cork to Thurles.

In the guards van travelled small calves tied up in sacks and when they got loose they caused consternation as did the ferrets who hid behind the mail bags having escaped from the boxes in which they were confined.

The weighing of salmon for export was a task which had to be dealt with in an exact manner because most often consignees gave only the weight of the salmon less the ice in which it was packaged on their consignment dockets On checking a big discrepancy in the true weights showed up. Charges had to be

The Man from the Railway

levied on the merchandise concerned and, of course, this provided extra revenue for the railway.

When decimal currency came in it caused much confusion and we had to come in on Sundays to be trained to use it. One old woman from Kerry who I met on a train said that she was optimistic that it would never reach her village.

There was a railway driver who was a keen angler and was always complaining that he never caught anything. One windy day his cap fell into the water. The flies caught onto it and when the cap came afloat there were five fish snared onto it. Another day he saw a baby otter grounded on the river bank. He put it back into the river and soon a huge salmon was landed at his feet. The mother otter had swam alongside with it in her mouth and dropped it in front of him. She seemed to be saying thanks.

The Man from the Railway

Every man to his own sport and hobbies and one of the most interesting groups arrived to us on the 'Pigeon Specials' The pigeon fanciers sent their cargo in baskets down from Belfast. We would take them off the train and write down where and when we released them. They would be timed when they got home and a winner decided. Some would never get home as they would get caught in wire or be eaten by hawks. On several occasions special trains came with attendants from Belfast to West Cork for gigantic races. To put it mildly the comings and goings of a railwayman's life were very varied.

The Man from the Railway

On the 16th May 1984 when I signed off in the duty book I had made the grade of Ticket Collector. In my forty eight years with the railway, man and boy, there had been so many changes. The rail company was now called Coras Iompair Eireann, train travel had changed dramatically and I was part of its history.

As I prepared to bid farewell I remembered back to the beginning of my career when I was on early duty. My route to the station brought me down the steps by St. Mary's Dominican Priory. One morning I met a little girl. She was standing at the door of her house, afraid to move because of a black labrador dog standing in front of her. I took her up the steps and she was able to proceed on her way to school. Her mother knew that I would be passing by regularly, so she told her daughter to 'wait for The Man from the Railway'. Some years later, when checking one of the Dublin to Cork trains, I was introduced by her mother to my little friend, now a young lady.

It's a small world, don't you think?